SONGS FROM THE
CENTER OF THE WELL

SONGS FROM THE CENTER OF THE WELL

Swami Chetanananda

RUDRA PRESS • Portland, Oregon

RUDRA PRESS
P.O. Box 13310
Portland, Oregon 97213
800-876-7798
www.rudrapress.com

Cover photo by Linda Saxton
Photograph of Author: Patricia Slote

Cover photo: Samadhi shrine of Chetanananda's guru, Rudi (Swami Rudrananda), Big Indian, New York, 1985.

Library of Congress Cataloging-in Publication Data

Chetanananda, Swami
     Songs from the center of the well / Swami Chetanananda. – Rev. ed.
        p.   cm.

     ISBN 978-0-915801-03-9
     1. Spiritual life. 2. Meditations.   I. Title
BL624.C453   1991   90-15561
291.4—dc20   CIP

Dedication

*In love itself there is no need, no absence of anything
no void.
When we find it inside, we discover we have enough for ourselves
and everybody else,
and we need go no further.
We become like a well;
we quench our own thirst
and have water enough for anyone who passes by.*

ABOUT THE AUTHOR

SWAMI CHETANANANDA ("Swamiji") is an American meditation master who has dedicated his life to promoting the experience of total-well being for his students and everyone around him. He is the founder of The Movement Center, a non-profit center for spiritual study and practice.

Swamiji is a powerful teacher with the capacity to transmit an immediate awareness of the state of intrinsic wellness at our core. With an understanding that spirituality transcends the confines of religious identity, he has the rare distinction of being a lineage holder in both the Hindu and Buddhist tantric traditions.

Swamiji's teachings center on how to live a deeply satisfying life. In this, his first book, his writings are a celebration of life, full of humor and compassion. The message is profoundly simple: life is nothing but the manifestation of the Divine, and that divinity lies within each human being. The title of this collection, Songs from the Center of the Well, refers to the role of a spiritual teacher – one who knows the source, taps the fountainhead, and endlessly quenches the thirst of those who stop to drink.

To hear talks and view videos of Swamiji, visit www.chetanananda.org.

PUBLISHER'S NOTE

It is with great pleasure and satisfaction that we present this collection of remarkable verse from the writings of Swami Chetanananda. They have been selected from the many pages of his work to represent the most powerful characteristics of the man himself – the embodiment of the mystical in the physical, the genuine love of life, the tremendous inner strength and insight, and the understanding that is at once fathomless and utterly simple.

These songs are the direct teachings of Swamiji. Any attempt to characterize them is very difficult – they are neither poetry nor prose, they do not sermonize nor eulogize, they fit no religious or literary mold. They are spoken directly from the heart about matters close to the heart. They are both deeply subtle and startlingly direct. Some give advice or guidance, some celebrate the beauty and power of life, some define the aspects of spirituality we so often misunderstand – surrender, grace, one's relationship to a teacher. Some simply cajole us into the happy knowledge that our lives are permeated by the divine, and that the greatest power and the greatest good lies within our own hearts.

Swamiji's teachings are rooted in the Tantric tradition passed on to him through the teachers in his lineage, the most recent of which are Swami Rudrananda, Swami Nityananda, and Swami Muktananda. The rich and powerful influence of the East is readily apparent, yet he writes with a Westerner's hand and listens with a Westerner's ear. In his work East authentically meets West, and the esoteric teachings of an ancient tradition spring to life. One continually finds parallels between the classical texts, so often difficult to understand, and the insights he articulates in everyday language. For those who know him this comes as no surprise; he *lives* what he teaches. Because he lives it, his articulation is not culture-bound, and he is free to write about it in a language we can understand.

Songs from the Center of the Well is a book to pick up again and again, to break open in a quiet moment, to take with you on a journey filled with uncertainty. To read it is to pause, take a new look at the world, and breathe a sigh of relief. One might go to the *Songs* as one goes to a trusted friend at a difficult time. We have read them many times, under many different circumstances, and each time we have found a freshness and insight that cheered and steadied us. It is our great joy to share this treasure with you, and to hope it brings you the peace and understanding it has brought to us.

Table of Contents

Songs From the Center of the Well

THE LOGIC OF LOVE

THE LOGIC OF LOVE

IN A SPIRITUAL LIFE, love is the sole motivator; love is synonymous with the power of life itself. Yet this love is mysterious, with a logic that often defies the logic of reason. Great spiritual people give when reason would have them withhold; they open when reason would have them withdraw. The logic of love calls for surrender and selflessness, and it produces respect and compassion.

The logic of love *can* be mastered; still, it is an unusual course of study. Unlike chemistry or calculus, it will never have a code of rules, because love demands a fresh response in every situation. Its ways are not easy to follow. The best way to learn about it is in the presence of one who has mastered it already. If you study such a person carefully, the subtlety and elegance behind the logic reveals itself, and your understanding is transformed.

THE LOGIC OF LOVE / *action*

In all things you do in this world, go carefully
and have it be your goal to remain at peace within yourself
no matter what.
Don't be ambitious to get everything done.
That will make you hungry and crazy.
It will destroy your ability to see your way.
When you find something to do, proceed with
profound detachment.
That means:
produce quality in the moment
and give the future to God.

THE LOGIC OF LOVE / *insight*

Stabilize your mind in the deep love and respect
that is the substance of your life and of life itself.
For you
the world will cease to be a confusing, frustrating,
disappointing place.
It will become permeated with magic and mystery and miracles.

THE LOGIC OF LOVE / *detachment*

Don't let your desires cloud your judgment.
Don't let your desires create unhappy marriages for you.
Concentrate on love.
Even if you have to live a very simple life,
even simple to the point of austerity,
you will not know it.
Love will be so full in your heart that nothing in the world
can seem austere.
It's only austere if we're bitter about it, if we feel we're
making some sacrifice.
If we're keeping score with God,
if we're saying, "OK God, I'm giving you this,
now what are you going to give me?"—
that's austerity.

THE LOGIC OF LOVE / *understanding*

A spiritual understanding means we hold no assumptions
about the level of our capacity.
It means
we don't have any ego-trip about how good we are
nor do we feel inferior.
We simply take each and every act in front of us
as an opportunity to explore the very substance of life.
Sitting in meditation and working in the world merge
because it is the same quality of life that we explore directly
when we sit
and explore again in every action we undertake.
Do this and you will elevate your understanding. Do this,
and every action will reflect the purity of your heart
and the maturity of your intelligence.

THE LOGIC OF LOVE / *surrender*

If you cannot surrender yourself to the process of life,
you are like a stream arguing with a rock.
Do you think a river comes up to a rock
and spends all its time trying to move it?
Of course not.
The stream encompasses the rock.
The rock becomes a feature of the stream.
In time the rock becomes smooth
and all its edges polished.
The radiance in its structure is revealed.

THE LOGIC OF LOVE / *others*

We're not here to judge people, we're here
to unlock them.
In unlocking people you will discover
in every single one
a vast amount of simple goodness.

THE LOGIC OF LOVE / *detachment*

Liberated people no longer worry about their future,
about their relationships, about their jobs.
They are concerned with functioning honestly
and with integrity in this moment and the next.
They are concerned with doing the work in front of them
not out of a need for recognition or wealth or power
but out of profound love and respect
for those people who surround them
and those forces that brought them here.
Such an awareness has to change our experience of this world.
Such an awareness has to allow for the unbroken presence of
happiness and beauty and enthusiasm and inspiration.

THE LOGIC OF LOVE / *discipline*

The whole purpose of austerity,
the whole purpose of discipline,
the whole purpose of yoga,
is that you should become strong inside.
Full of love and respect, full of wisdom and compassion,
but completely strong.
So you don't get seduced by any worldly deception.
So you don't get taken in by your own
or anybody else's delusions.

THE LOGIC OF LOVE / *surrender*

When we live a life of surrender
we are simply living intelligently:
living with great integrity and compassion,
with balance and patience and foresight.
It is not that we surrender everything we think is fun
or we think is a bad habit or we think is unspiritual.
It is an issue of common sense.
You may put your hand in the lawn mower once
but you don't do it twice.

THE LOGIC OF LOVE / *freedom*

By looking inside, a person becomes free;
free from the constraints of this body and biology,
free from the endless web of want and need,
free from every kind of limitation and fear.
At that point we gain the strength to look out and see in
everything, no matter how horrific or terrifying,
the same gracious force that lies within.
Such a vision has to transform us.
Such a vision has to bring inner peace.

THE LOGIC OF LOVE / *understanding*

Spiritual understanding means having the right priorities
and having a genuine commitment to those priorities.
Living a spiritual understanding means expressing those
priorities
in the hot moments;
the moments when it really counts.

THE LOGIC OF LOVE / *reality*

Anyone who is proud is confused.
What is this thing you walk around in that you are proud of?
Dust.
The body is dust.
Actions without spirit are less than air,
less than wind.
It's only spirit that has substance. It's only spirit
that has contact.
It's only spirit that has longevity.
Everything else is dust.
To be proud of dust is like taking clay from a diamond mine.

THE LOGIC OF LOVE / *choice*

There are two ways to live.
There's a life of conflict
or a life of surrender.

THE WELL

The Well

In this analogy, the guru is the well, and the water is the power of life itself, love, grace, Shakti, God, the inner lover. Like a true spiritual teacher, the well asks for nothing in return, it simply *is* — an endless, life-giving supply requiring only that you fashion a container and make the effort of drawing.

It is *grace* that brings a student to the well, and it is grace that sustains his connection, through the well, to the source of life itself.

THE WELL / *grace*

In the harmony and balance of life
whatever we put on the scales:
our caring, our commitment, our sacrifice, our dedication,
our devotion,
always has to be equaled.
Grace does the balancing.
It unfolds the opportunity to become uplifted, to grow,
to endlessly expand our horizons.
In this way, we merge into the universe.
We become one with God.
And our vision is that everything is God.
Then the whole world from day one to the end of time
becomes a spontaneous momentary flash
of divine love.

THE WELL / *shaktipat*

Shaktipat brings the intimate experience of the unity
in the fabric of being.
Any fabric is nothing but the relationship of threads.
If one of them breaks, the entire piece must unravel.
The power of shaktipat
awakens us to our place in that fabric
and we become thoughtful and considerate in weaving our part.
Because of our awareness
we take great care not to break any threads.

THE WELL / *the teacher*

In relationship to a spiritual teacher,
the concepts of close and distant
have no meaning.
The teaching itself is beyond close and distant.
It is not from the body or personality of a teacher that you hope
to learn:
when the body turns to dust
what will you have learned?
It is only the inner lover we wish to grow close to.
The teacher is one who knows the inner lover
as well as it is possible to know him.
He can introduce you. He can plant the seed.
From there
you must tend the garden.

THE WELL / *grace*

It is your feeling and your good actions that provoke grace.
If you are stingy and fickle,
you are like a small pipe, rusty on the inside;
not much water can run through.
If it is grace you seek in your life,
just change the plumbing.
A larger pipe automatically carries more water.

THE WELL / *grace*

In the same sense that the farmer throws seed everywhere,
so grace is present in vast abundance for everyone.
But of course the seed only grows in ground that has been
cultivated,
ground that is plowed and ready to receive it.
The seed reaches maturity in the field that has been tended
carefully.
In the same sense that Shiva and Shakti are one,
self-effort and grace are interpenetrated completely.
Because you make the sacrifice from within,
the self-effort and grace merge
and give forth a mature spiritual state.

THE WELL / *detachment*

The greatest power, the highest attainment, a person can have
is detachment.
When nothing in this world has power over you,
you are a liberated being.
All of the miracles of great beings manifest because of
detachment.
Their hearts are continuously open.
They have no defenses.
They are nothing but open channels for the manifestation
of morality and responsibility,
of serenity and love.

WISDOM

WISDOM

WISDOM REFERS TO the insight and understanding that come from authentic spiritual practice. One learns it through one's sustained contact with the inner Self. It has nothing to do with do's and don'ts. There is no dogma or doctrine that encompasses it. Its manifestation changes with every circumstance. The only way to attain it is through persistent effort toward growth. The only practice necessary to gain it is surrender.

WISDOM / *quality*

You can study all the scripture in the world,
you can know every religious tradition and recite every page from
every holy book,
you can be excellent in every meditation technique and all the
austerities,
but if you don't know from within yourself what quality is
and you don't value it,
you cannot know the Self.
Everything that has ever been written is to inspire people to
make the difficult, demanding, disturbing, uncomfortable,
conscious effort
every day
to be a deeply quality human being.

WISDOM / *growth*

Growing is cultivating and sustaining
the fire of our own inner Spirit.
It is not something that allows us to become comfortable.
It allows us to become deeply peaceful.
The inner fire is our guiding light;
without it we are lost people.
When we feed into that fire the thickness of our prejudices,
our desires, our egotism, our point of view,
its guiding light becomes very, very bright.
It illuminates the selfless inner Self,
the universal point of view,
the Absolute.

WISDOM / *attitude*

Come to meditation and open yourself inside to all of life.
Open your creative energy to the activity you undertake
every day.
From that basic opening, simply and quietly and introspectively
move through the world
performing the different acts you have to perform.
Refrain from the tendency to become negative in any respect.
Allow the power of creative energy to work its magic around you.
After a while your mind matures
and you understand fully the nature of this creative process.
Then you will surely be freed from all the limitations
of this life.

WISDOM / *effort*

Anyone established in the process of creative expression
experiences the ecstatic promotion it brings
and knows what work it is to acquire this skill
and the strength it asks
to remain in that joy.
It's work;
that's all there is.

WISDOM / *effort*

There are eight million excuses for us
to be less than we are.
It's like the work of a farmer who clears a virgin forest—
there are eight million chuckholes to fall into.
There is only one way to realize your potential:
don't accept any excuses.
Take the responsibility every day;
take it whether you like it or not. This becomes your life.
This also becomes your harvest.

WISDOM / *pain*

When, because of love, we face the painful situations:
we don't run, we don't turn our backs,
we don't shrink or make excuses, we face them,
in that moment we are totally transformed.

WISDOM / *surrender*

Surrender brings out that vibration of perfect, pure
intelligence. In doing so, it brings harmony.
It unfolds the direction of our creative energy.
There is never any lessening of anything.
To enter a state of surrender is to let
go of all the obstructions, the imbalance, the obstacles,
and yield to the pulsation of pure conscious energy.
There, perfect intelligence and pure capacity merge.
In that state our earthly will is dissolved
and the divine will manifests.

WISDOM / *surrender*

Only a person established in surrender attains the
vision of the infinite.
Surrender of our earthly will is the essence of yoga,
the essence of spirituality.
It is the essence of God Realization—
something not easily accomplished.

WISDOM / *growth*

A person matures by making a conscious creative effort
in a positive direction.
All faults, misunderstandings, and confusions
are simply absorbed into that creative flow.
There is no need to address yourself to correcting faults.
Trying to correct faults is like trying to put five fingers
on five fleas.
Every time you correct one fault,
another one pops up someplace else, and then when you go to
correct that fault,
the first one is back.
Keep established in the creative energy, and faults fall away
naturally, effortlessly.

WISDOM / *meditation*

There are many times when it's necessary to do your homework,
to sit for a long time and deeply ask
and ask and ask
until you really feel that you are asking from the deepest place.
You create a vibration, a feeling,
a kind of intensity from deeply within you
that begins to condense and then expand
and change the chemistry of your whole body.
When you don't reach from a deep place within yourself,
how is anything going to happen?
What can grow in rocks and sand?

WISDOM / *devotion*

The highest discipline of all is devotion
but not devotion that comes and goes:
permanence in devotion.

WISDOM / *burning*

Burning takes place when attachment starts to get severed
or some error starts to unwind,
some crossed wire
or wrong thinking.
When we see it, we should take responsiblity for it.
Everybody defends themselves.
You think you can't possibly be wrong, it has to be somebody
else's fault, somebody else's error.
With this attitude,
you will slow burn for the next twenty million years.
That slow burn is called worldly life.
But when you take responsibility for your behavior,
your mistakes, your wrong thinking,
and correct them,
then burning doesn't take long
and the light given off is brilliant.

WISDOM / *effort*

Because we over and over and over again,
in the face of disappointment and frustration and
disillusionment and challenge and distraction and diversion and
tension and doubt and fear,
persevere,
slowly we ripen and mature as spiritual beings
and merge consciously
into the Absolute.

WISDOM / *freedom*

When you merge all that is voluntary about you
with the very foundation of your existence,
which is involuntary,
freedom comes automatically.
When you withdraw all the attachments,
wash away the fears and tensions and problems,
you grant yourself
a peaceful, joyous experience.
You open yourself to the depths of your being.
As long as we have to struggle with the world,
with our feelings of adequacy and inadequacy and uncertainty,
as long as there is the continuing battle with our own ego,
there is no room for spirituality.
There has to come a point in our lives
when quietly, deeply
we accept ourselves.

WISDOM

The only thing that really grows
is our awareness of our own nature.

THE INNER FRIEND

THE INNER FRIEND

THE SELF, GOD, the Divine, Shiva, the Guru. All of these are synonyms for the inner friend. He/She is the power behind all life, eternal and changeless, the source of every kind of joy and satisfaction. Contact with the inner friend is what every human longs for, although most don't recognize it. Distance from the inner friend is what brings about all suffering. When you understand these two simple truths from every pore of your being, liberation is within your grasp.

THE INNER FRIEND / *perfection*

If you had a friend who was perfect,
who was beautiful and brilliant and wealthy and charming
and everything else,
you would want to spend all your time with that friend.
Each of us has such a friend within us.
When we get over our insecurities, when we are open enough
to build a rapport with that friend,
slowly we discover an extraordinary capacity,
and slowly we claim it for our own.

THE INNER FRIEND / *meditation*

If there is a dust storm inside, then how will you know the inner friend?
It is like walking next to someone in a dark fog;
you won't be able to see him.
Even though he never leaves you, you don't see him.
Only when the light of understanding dawns within us
do we clearly perceive our inner friend.
Then all our searching in the world,
our yearning and our burning,
is put to an end.
Then meditation is not a struggle,
it is not even an effort.
Meditation is just being with our inner friend.

THE INNER FRIEND / *confusion*

All the trouble in our lives is the result of one simple
confusion.
That is the confusion over the inner lover.
We search outside everywhere. We look here and there and say
"Is this the one?" "When I leave this one
will *that* be the one?"
Yet, the One we are searching for is always inside.
All of our coming and going and planning and struggling
and scheming and hoping and clinging
in whatever desire we reach for,
comes from the single, all-powerful need
for intimacy with the inner lover.

THE INNER FRIEND / *meditation*

When you are with someone you love very much,
you can talk and it is pleasant,
but the reality is not in the conversation.
It is simply in the being together.
Meditation is the highest form of prayer. In it you are so close
to God
that you don't need to say a thing—it's just great to be
together.

THE INNER FRIEND / *awakening*

There is no suppressing the mind.
You can't stop it, it just keeps going.
But there is quieting the mind.
It quiets due to the power of the Self.
When we awaken to the Self, a great stillness comes about.
Every question of what we want or what we think we need
or what we think has to change
is put to an end.
Then the mind becomes a precision tool. We use it with skill
and no longer can it harm us
or anybody else.

THE INNER FRIEND / *awareness*

In the same sense that breathing brings oxygen to the body and
carries out poisonous wastes,
our awareness of the divine force
purifies.
Just as breath is life to the cells,
this divine force is the Life of a human being.
It gives movement and strength,
it brings inspiration and removes all obstacles.
A person established in the simple awareness of this force
ultimately experiences wave upon wave
of pure bliss.

THE INNER FRIEND / *awareness*

Certainly you can't attain anything great by running away from
what's hard
or chasing after what looks interesting.
You attain great spirituality when your mind is stable.
Your mind is stable only through your continuous,
conscious awareness of the pulsation of the divine force.
This pulsation is the essence of mantra.
It is the essence of breath.
It is dynamic stillness.
It is the pathless path.
To take it
you need no technique, no austerity, no ritual. You need only the
pure unbroken awareness of the divine pulsation.
Listen for it
and it will set you free.

THE WORLD

THE WORLD

THE WORLD IS everything manifest. It is not an illusion, but it is not the substance of reality. It is like a play, and we are simply acting out parts. It has a certain magic, and we should learn to play our parts very well, but we should never come under its spell.

Spiritual people use their experience in the world to learn discrimination, compassion, and freedom from judgment and fear. They are equally happy with austerity or opulence. They move through the world with great detachment, seeing it as nothing other than an opportunity for growth.

THE WORLD / *the goddess Kundalini*

When the goddess Kundalini sleeps in the base of the spine
it's because she's gotten tired watching the same movie
over and over.
She is stuck at the movie of your problems and anxieties
and concerns and worries and desires.
It goes on over and over and over and over again.
And she just goes to sleep.
Wouldn't you?
As she sleeps, we forget who we are and what we are all about.
We lose touch with our aspirations and our ideals.
We become afraid of change and resist it.
We suspect other people and feel insecure.
Struggle arises everywhere as we try to grab hold of something
we haven't got
or hold onto something we think we have.
Shaktipat changes all that.
Shaktipat proclaims the end of the movie.
It turns on the lights
and everybody who was asleep wakes up and says,
"Gee, that was boring. Time to go home."
All the lights come on.
The goddess wakes up and remembers her true nature.

THE WORLD / *experience*

No experience in this world
has any value other than the value we ourselves give it.
You can talk about good experiences and bad experiences and
painful experiences and pleasant experiences;
but all experience is just experience.
It has no positive or negative value.
It is our own feeling that gives it whatever value it has.
Open your mind and all experience becomes extraordinary.
Even pain becomes extraordinary. Even in loss
we are enhanced.

THE WORLD / *success and failure*

If you do a quality job
whatever comes in the world, just comes.
Whatever comes,
be it wealth or poverty or ease or difficulty,
it will never take away your integrity or self-respect.
It will never undermine you.
It will never cause you a moment's unrest.
Whether what comes is opulence or fame or fortune or
utter, stark austerity,
it is nothing but a manifestation of the quality
that you treasure above everything else.

THE WORLD / *the stage*

To a person established in the Self this life is like a play.
We have taken on a role that we act out.
We try to play our role very well—we take it seriously. We do
it well, with feeling,
but not with the idea that this is the only role we will play.
At the end of the day we walk away from it,
we take off our make-up and we settle down.
We meet the Self and we are at ease.

THE WORLD / *delusion*

Simple, pure situations become polluted
because we try to get some angle on them.
We try to grasp something about them.
There is nothing to grasp.
Life at its core is fundamentally simple, utterly uncomplicated.
It is only our tensions that pollute it.
Open your own heart
and you will see the purity in all things.

THE WORLD / *thoughts*

Thoughts are nothing but the movement of conscious energ
just as the waves on the ocean's surface
are nothing but the movement of the ocean.
The waves aren't different from the ocean,
neither are the thoughts different from consciousness.
Just as the waves aren't solid
and don't have any substance separate from the ocean,
neither are any of these thoughts real
or independent from pure consciousness.
And just as the waves of the ocean come and go
and the movement is ceaseless,
so too, the thoughts that arise are fleeting.
Don't build your house on them.
The foundation will not hold.

THE WORLD / *tensions*

Tensions are inherent in everything.
They are not in themselves bad things. They are part of
life's beauty.
A person skilled in the art of life works with the tensions
in people and circumstances, and molds from them
extraordinary creative activity.

THE WORLD / *thoughts*

That thoughts and feelings arise and subside
is the ordinary nature of individual mind.
This should not cloud the inner sky of pure consciousness.
When you walk down a street
do you greet every person you pass
and listen to their life story?
Do you stop and argue about right of way?
No.
Let the thoughts and feelings go by.
It is only your confused idea that they should not be there in
the first place
that causes them to stay around
and causes you to doubt yourself.

THE WORLD / *the stage*

The world is simply a theatre in which your innermost,
conscious being unfolds its drama.
And while you are a player, an actress, an actor,
you are the director first.
If you could remember that
you would know the state of a liberated person,
you would know the strength of Shiva himself.
You are the actor and the enjoyer, the experiencer and
the experienced.
And you can do it with ease
because you know in the not too distant future
the lights are going to come up and the play will be over
and you will be free to go home.

THE WORLD / *right effort*

Right effort means living a simple and disciplined life.
If you have a railroad train
even if you have a big fire in the furnace,
without a top on the boiler all the steam escapes and you don't
move an inch.
So also, if you are dissipating your resources
what progress can be made?

THE WORLD / *the mind*

The same mind that seeks a grand concept,
the same mind that grasps for the meaning of the whole,
the same mind that wishes to possess the secrets of life,
is the mind that blocks us from Realization.
It is the mind that obstructs.
Realization is a lived-through experience.
It is not a commitment to a philosophy.
Philosophies are words and ideas, nothing more.
Let them be your tools, not your limitations.
The hammer and drill are not the whole house
nor are they the whole story of carpentry.

THE WORLD / *delusion*

If you clean the soot from the chimney of a glass lamp
you will have no trouble seeing your way.
The light will shine brightly.
It is only the soot that obstructs—it's never that the light has
gone out.
The soot is all the things we want
and all the things we're mad we didn't get.
When the soot is cleaned, the light shines.
In that light, where is there any darkness?
In that light,
where is there any need?
When that light shines,
how can we think there is something missing?

THE WORLD / *perfection*

Perfection is not a state
in which you arrive knowing all the answers
to every question.
Perfection is a state where upon arriving
you experience complete happiness and complete peace
just as you are.

The Nityananda Institute

THE NITYANANDA INSTITUTE, headquartered in Cambridge, Massachusetts, is dedicated to the active practice of a spiritual life based on the teachings of Swami Chetanananda. The Institute (formerly the Rudrananda Ashram) is named for the Indian saint Bhagavan Nityananda of Ganeshpuri, who is its wellspring and inspiration. However, both Chetanananda and his guru, Swami Rudrananda (Rudi) were born Americans, and it is this rich fusion of East and West that gives the Institute its unique character. Even though Chetanananda's teaching is deeply rooted in the rich traditions of Tantrism, it is completely Western in expression. He speaks in the language of America, he is as familiar with rock and roll as with the Rig Veda; like Rudi before him, Chetanananda is the embodied proof that cultural affiliation is no barrier to the highest understanding.

The Institute has many facets: a community of over a hundred residents; a full schedule of hatha yoga classes; twice-daily meditation sessions (introductory course required); periodic workshops in meditation techniques, relaxation techniques, and health enhancement; programs of art, music, and dance; quarterly weekend Retreats; public Satsang programs on Sunday mornings; and a wide range of publications produced by its publishing house, *Rudra Press*.